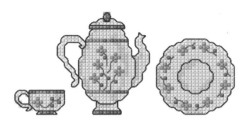

CROSS STITCH MOTIF SERIES 3

BORDERS

300 New Cross Stitch Motifs

Tuva Publishing
www.tuvayayincilik.com

Address: Merkez Mah. Çavuşbaşı Cad. No:71
Çekmeköy / Istanbul 34782 - TURKEY
Tel: 9 0216 642 62 62

Cross Stitch Motif Series 3 / Borders

First Print: 2012 / September, Istanbul
Second Print: 2013 / April, Istanbul
Third Print: 2013 / December, Istanbul
Fourth Print: 2014 / September, Istanbul

All Global Copyrights Belongs To
Tuva Tekstil San. ve Dış Tic. Ltd. Şti.

Content: Cross Stitch

Editor in Chief: Ayhan DEMİRPEHLİVAN
Project Editor: Kader DEMİRPEHLİVAN
Designer: Maria DIAZ
Technical Advisor: K. Leyla ARAS
Graphic Design: Ömer ALP, Büşra ESER
Asistant: Kevser BAYRAKÇI

ISBN: 978-605-5647-31-5

Printing House
Bilnet Matbaacılık ve Yayıncılık A.Ş.

Mouliné
Stranded Cotton Art. 117

●	798
✕	823
╱	823

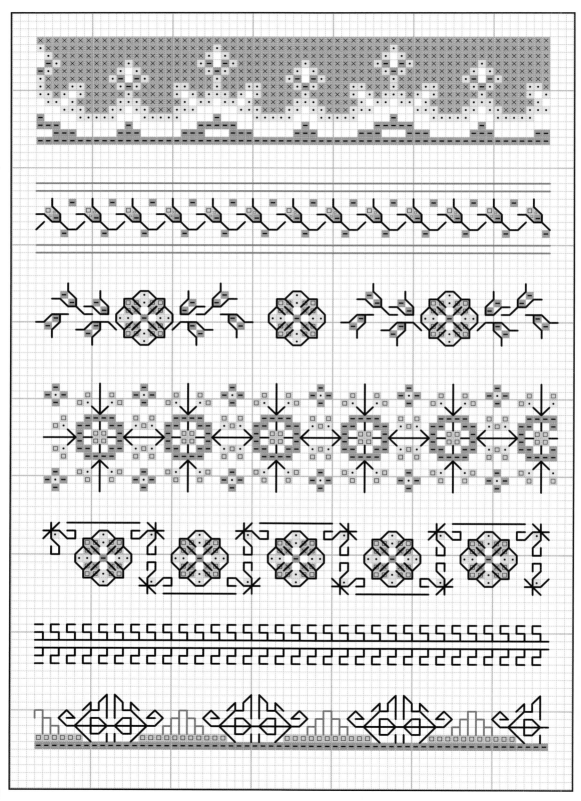

8

Mouliné
Stranded Cotton Art. 117

■	310
–	676
✕	817
╱	817

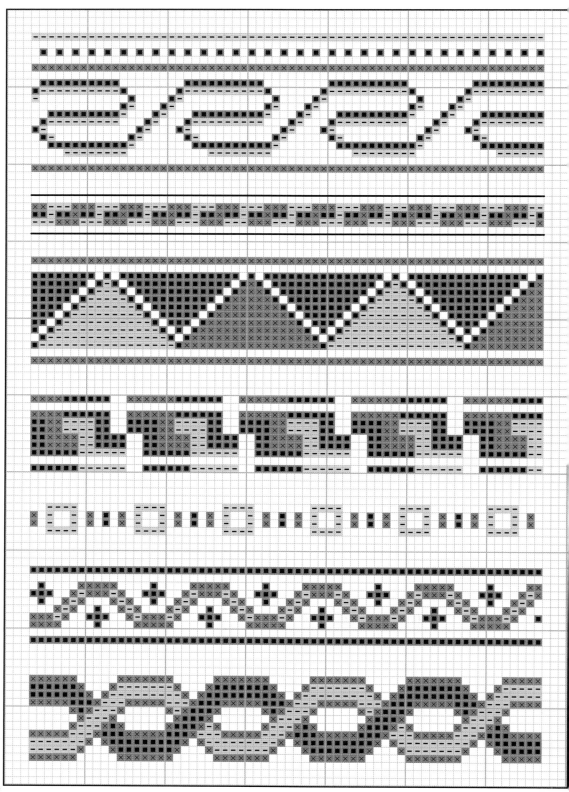

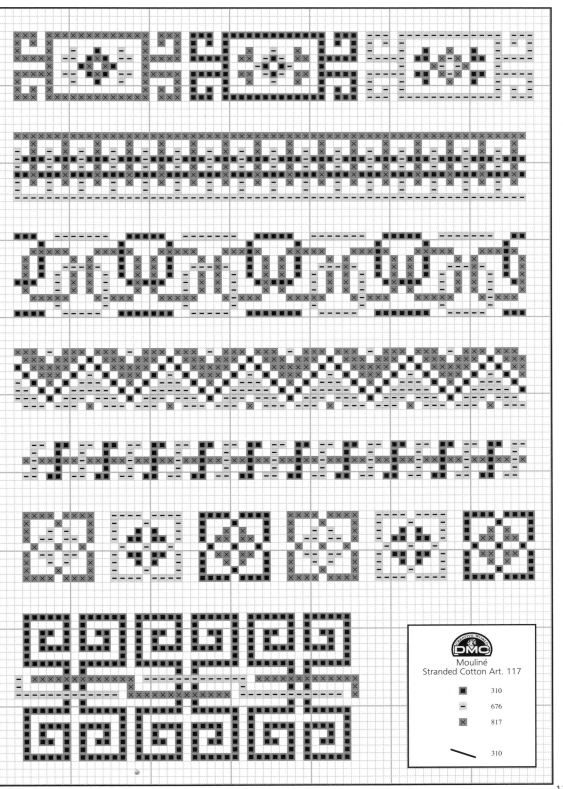

DMC
Mouliné
Stranded Cotton Art. 117

■	310
−	676
⊠	817
╱	310

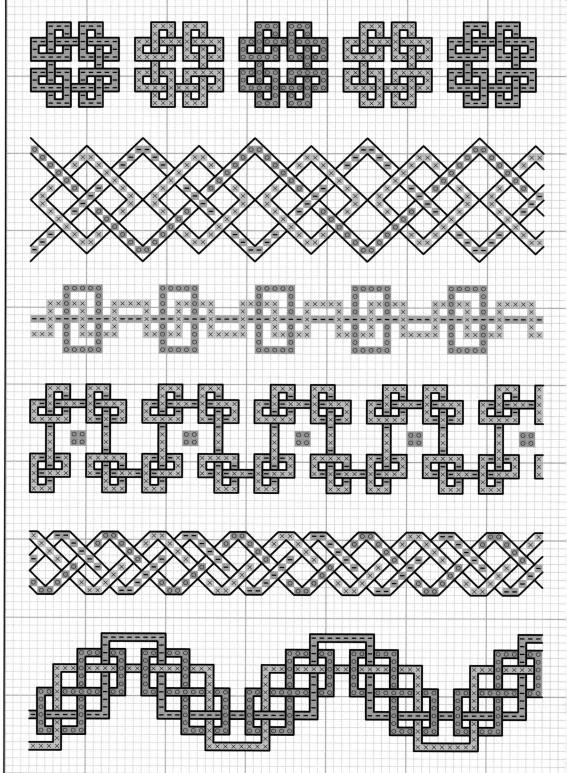

14

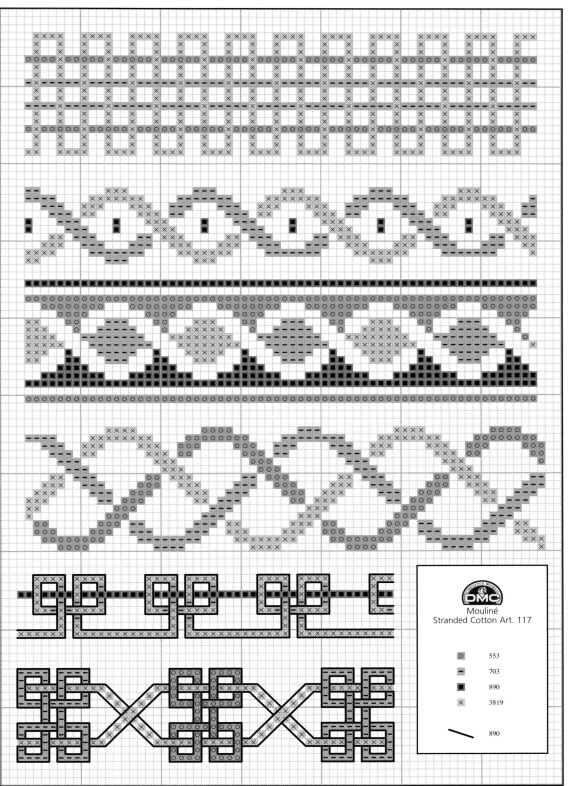

DMC
Mouliné
Stranded Cotton Art. 117

◎	553
−	703
■	890
×	3819

／ 890

15

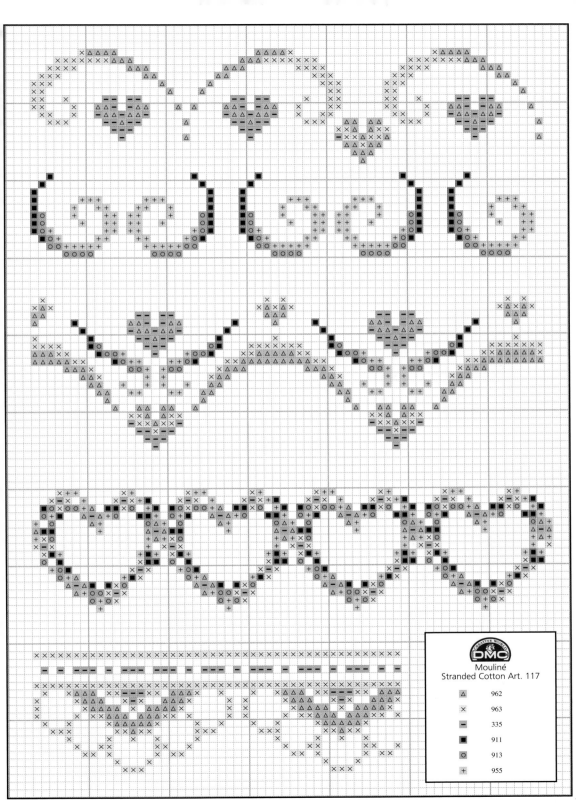

Mouliné
Stranded Cotton Art. 117

△	962
✗	963
−	335
◼	911
⊙	913
+	955

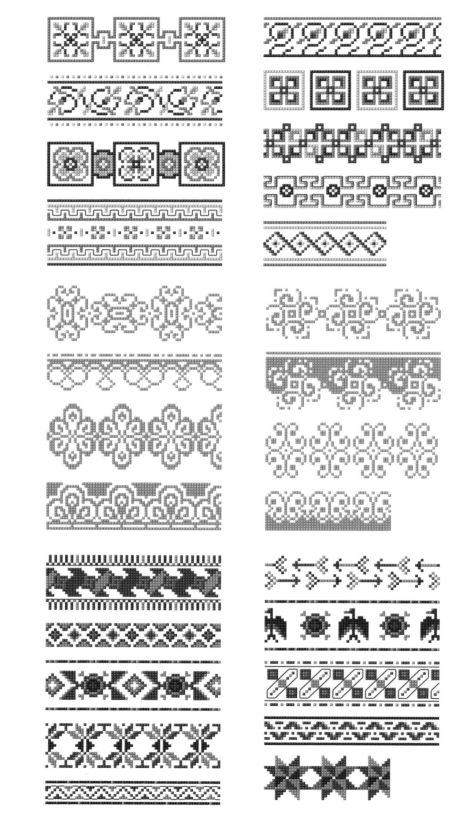

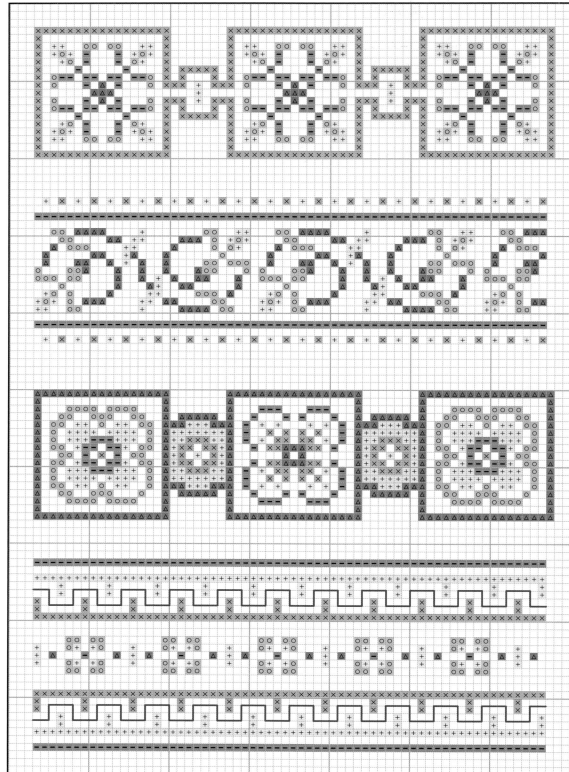

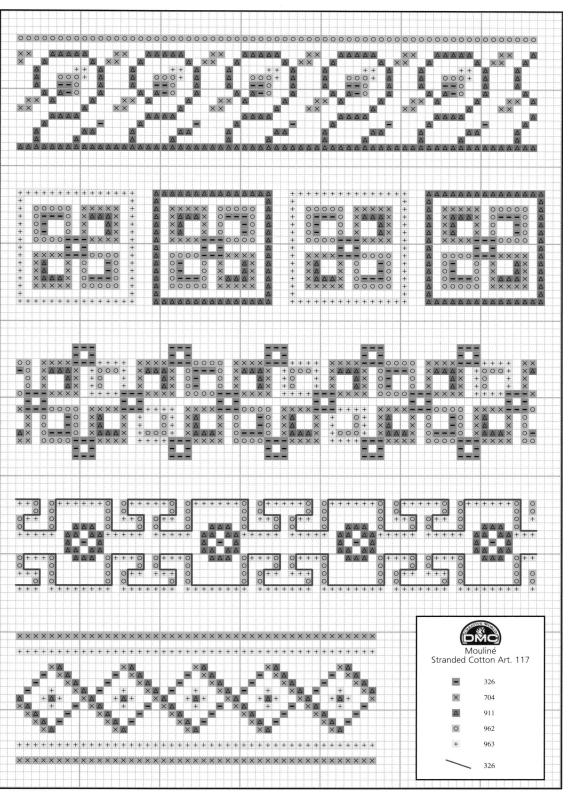

DMC
Mouliné
Stranded Cotton Art. 117

—	326
×	704
▲	911
○	962
+	963
╱	326

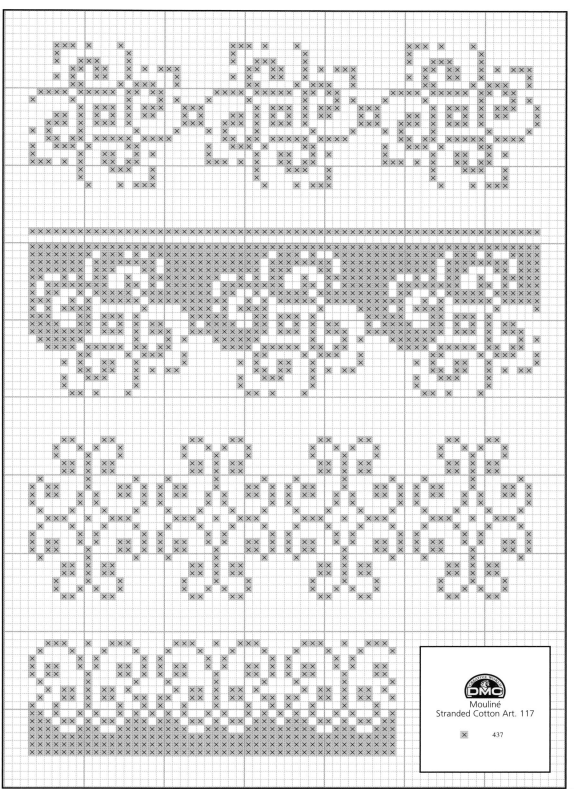

DMC
Mouliné
Stranded Cotton Art. 117

× 437

23

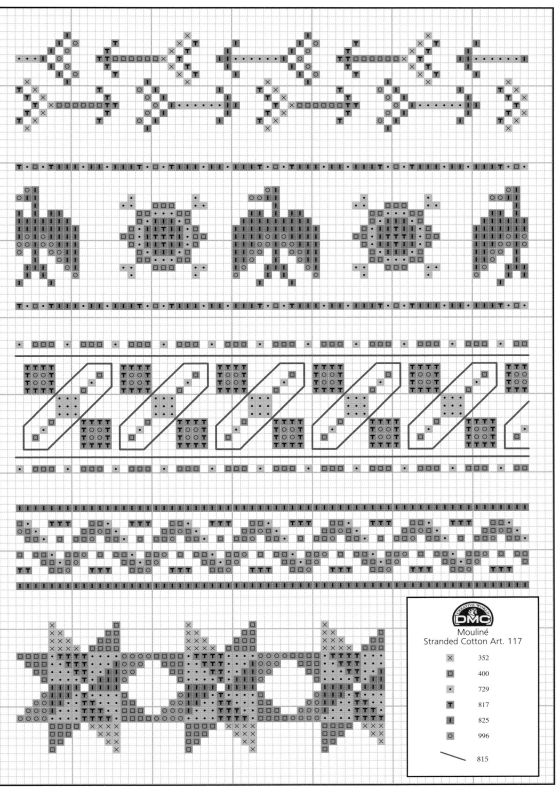

DMC
Mouliné
Stranded Cotton Art. 117

✕	352
▢	400
·	729
T	817
I	825
◎	996
╱	815

DMC
Mouliné
Stranded Cotton Art. 117

I	321
◎	552
•	554
✕	799
T	820

321

820

27

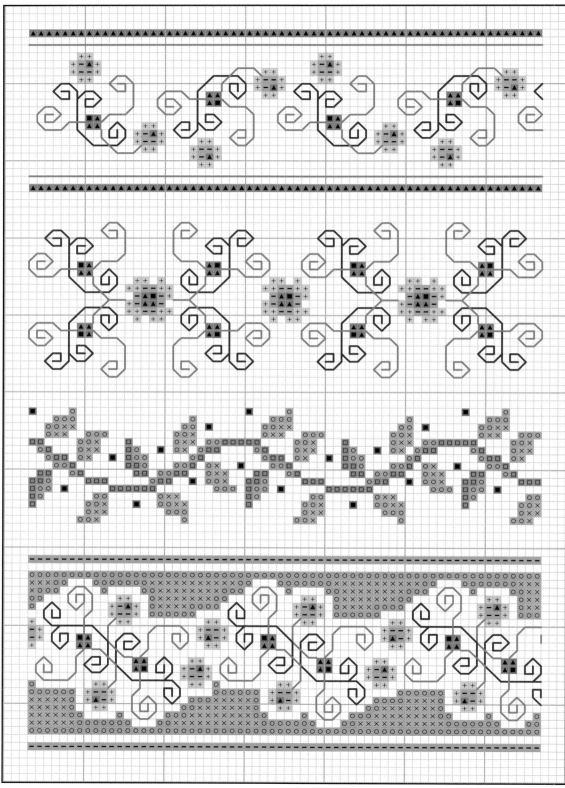

DMC
CREATIVE WORLD
Mouliné
Stranded Cotton Art. 117

■	154
•	165
▣	501
✕	704
▲	915
◉	3347
▬	3607
+	3609

╱	154
╱	501
╱	704

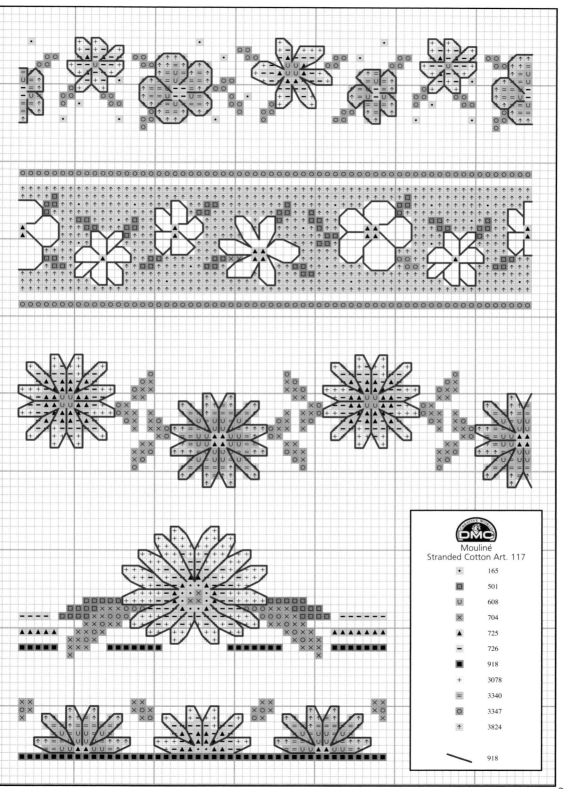

•	165
▣	501
U	608
×	704
▲	725
−	726
■	918
+	3078
=	3340
○	3347
↑	3824

DMC
Mouliné
Stranded Cotton Art. 117

╱ 918

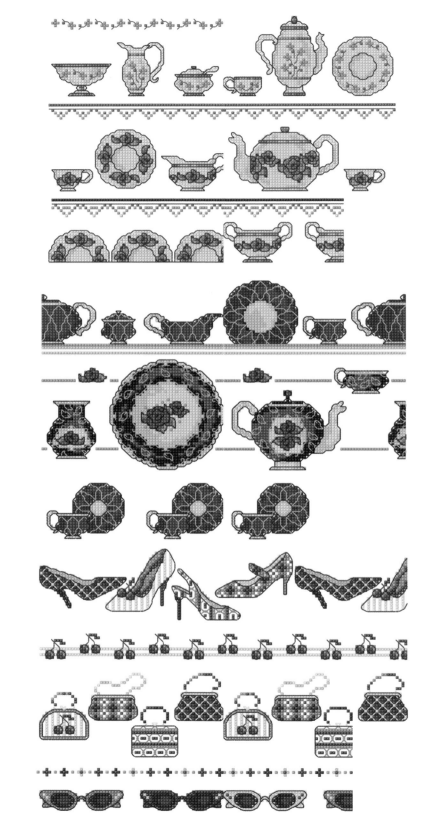

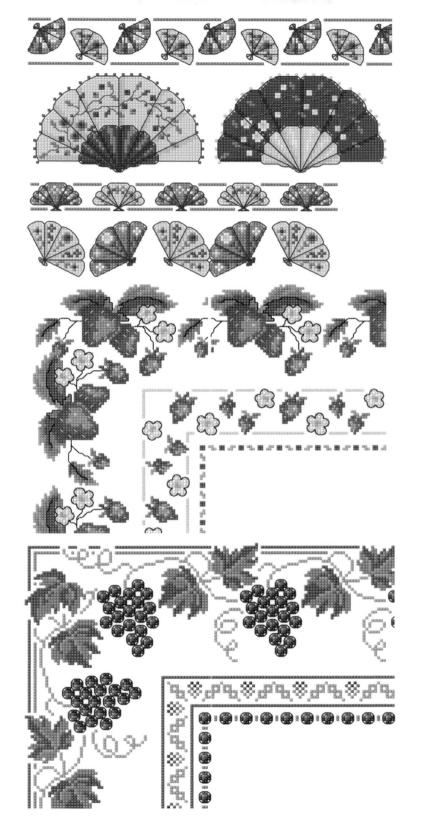

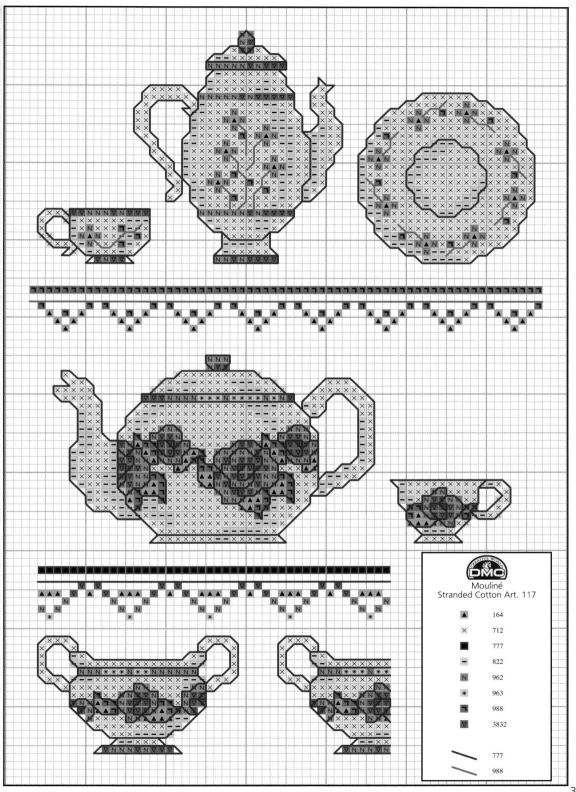

Mouliné
Stranded Cotton Art. 117

▲	164
✕	712
■	777
−	822
N	962
✳	963
◪	988
▽	3832
╱	777
╱	988

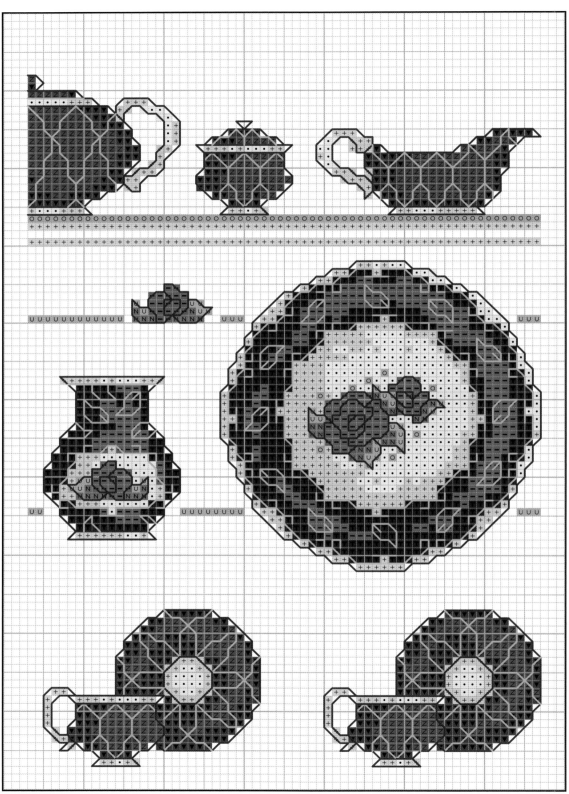

DMC	
Mouliné	
Stranded Cotton Art. 117	
U	164
Z	321
O	437
·	712
+	739
■	791
Y	816
N	988
−	3807
/	E3852
/	844

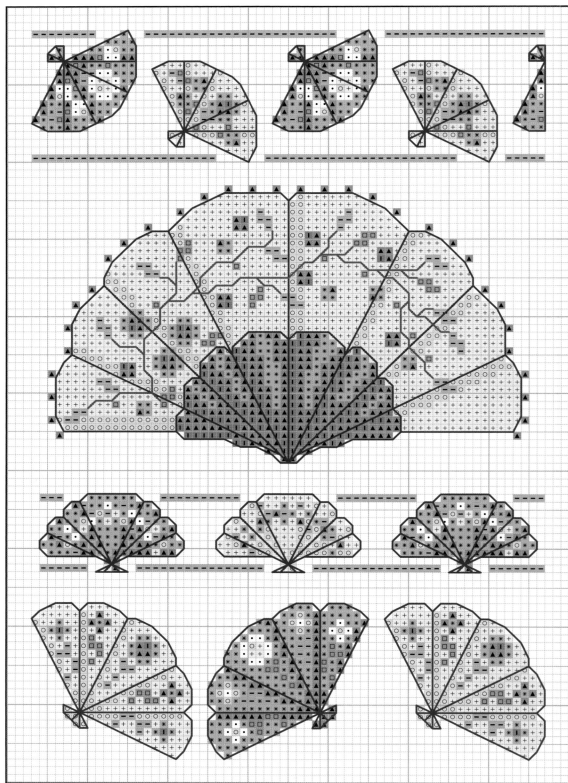

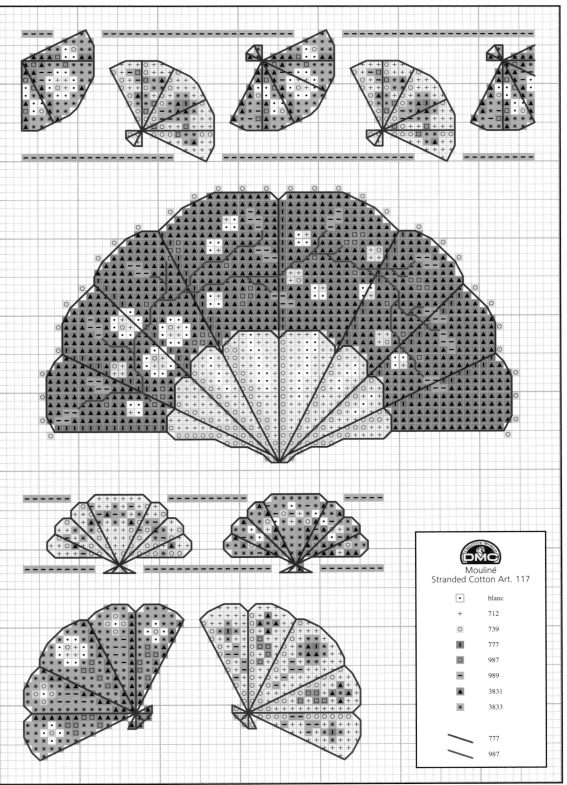

DMC
Mouliné
Stranded Cotton Art. 117

·	blanc
+	712
o	739
I	777
▢	987
—	989
▲	3831
∗	3833
╱	777
╱	987

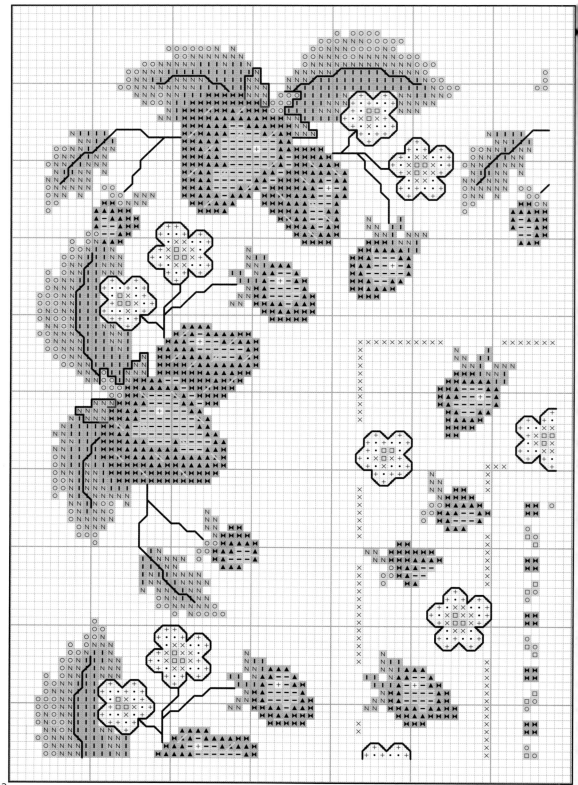

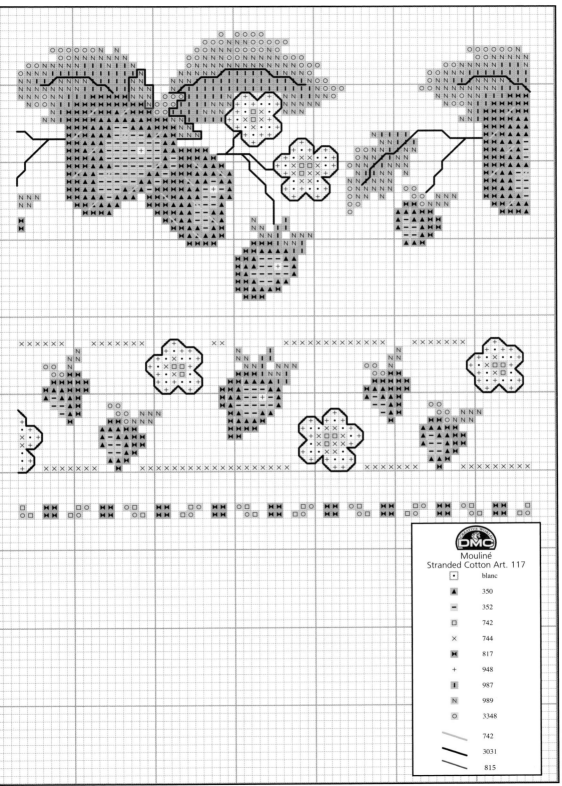

DMC

Mouliné
Stranded Cotton Art. 117

Symbol	Color
·	blanc
▲	350
−	352
□	742
×	744
◨	817
+	948
ı	987
N	989
o	3348
╱	742
╱	3031
╱	815

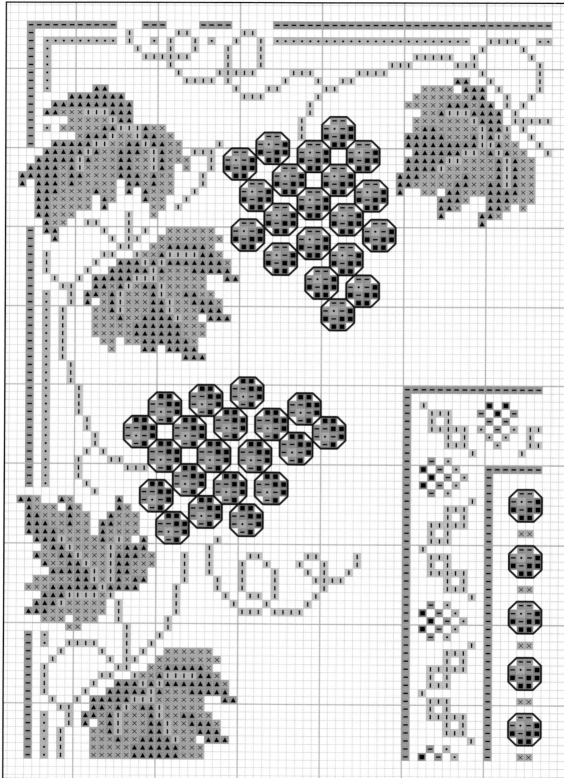

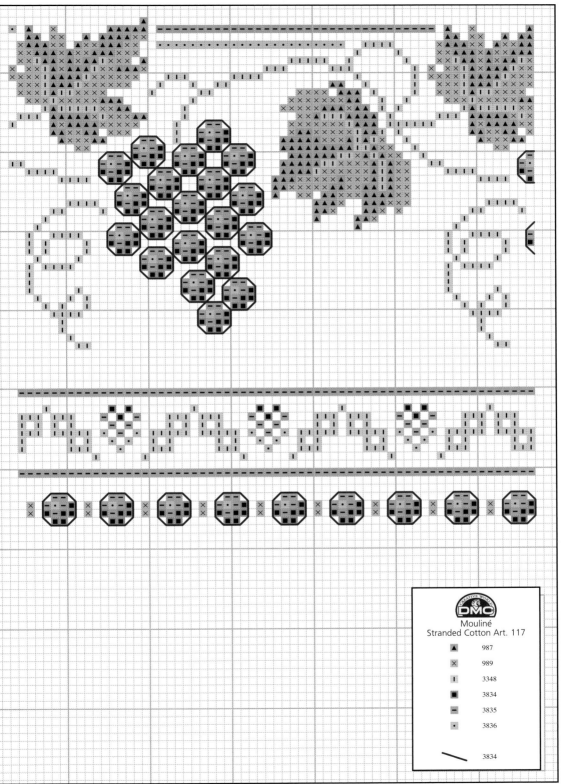

DMC
Mouliné
Stranded Cotton Art. 117

▲	987
×	989
I	3348
■	3834
−	3835
▪	3836

| ╱ | 3834 |

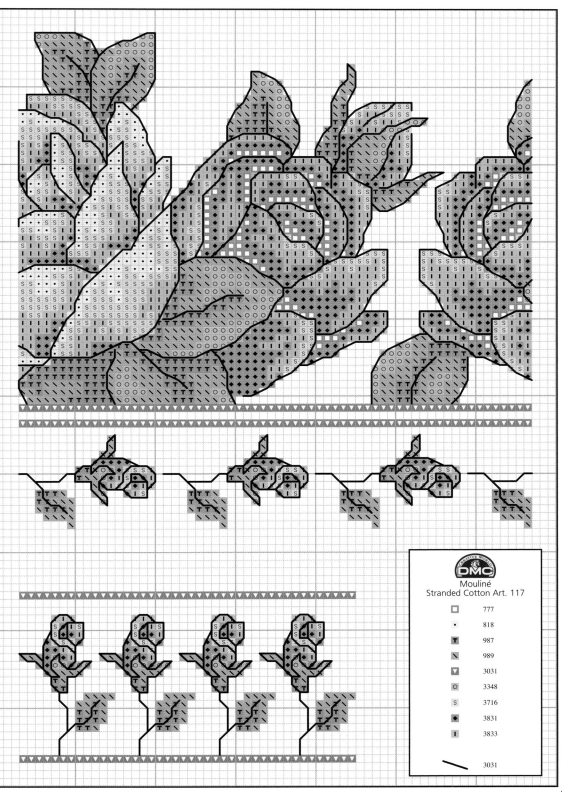

□	777	
·	818	
T	987	
◣	989	
▽	3031	
○	3348	
S	3716	
◆	3831	
I	3833	
╱	3031	

Mouliné
Stranded Cotton Art. 117

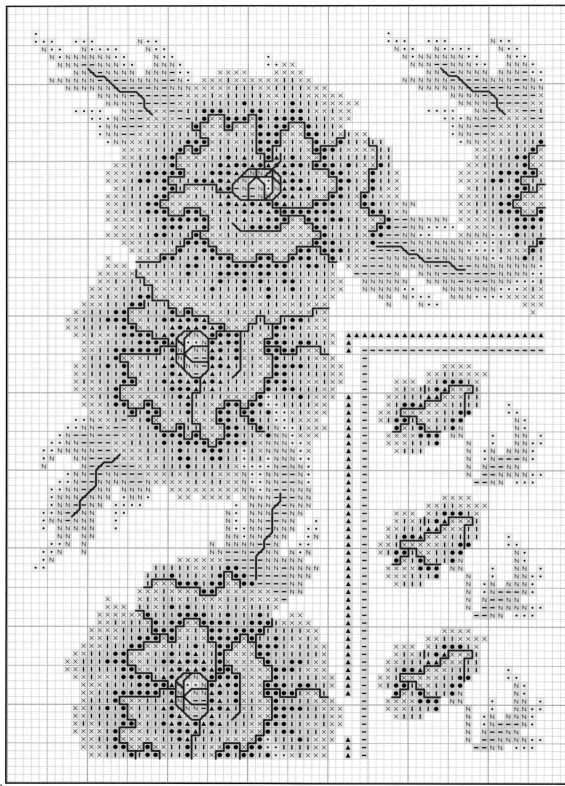

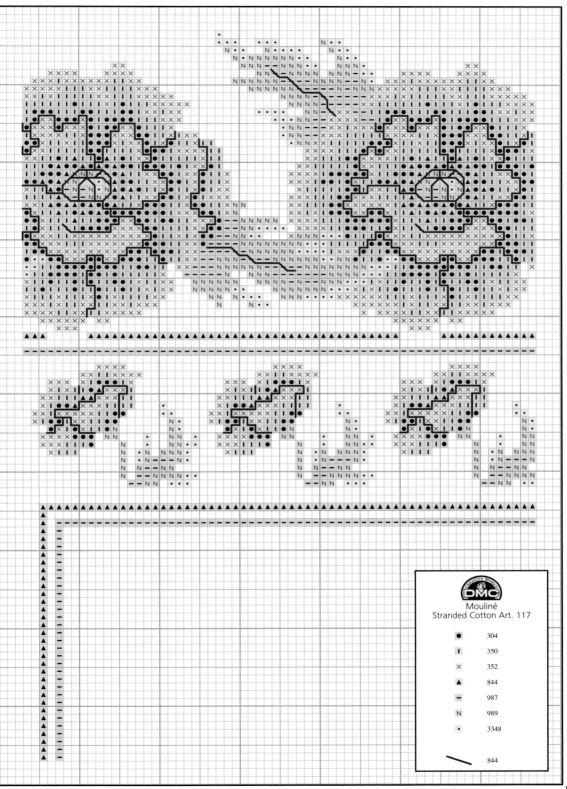

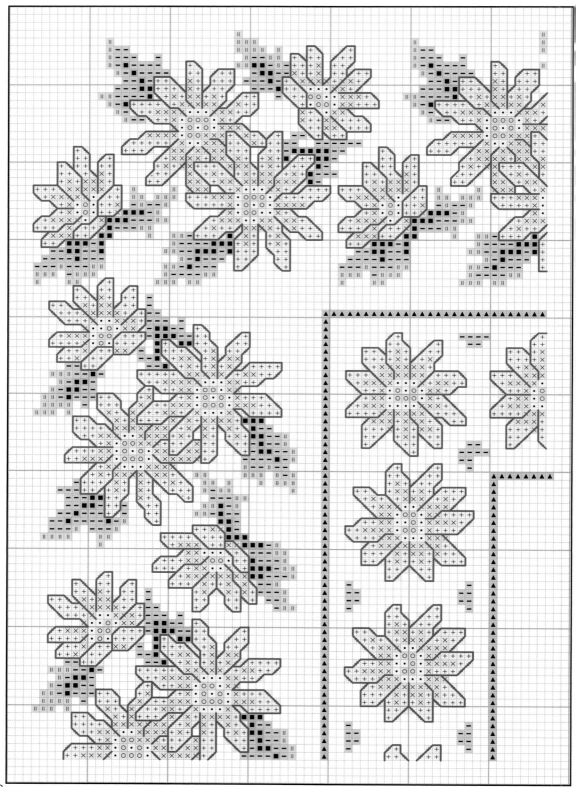

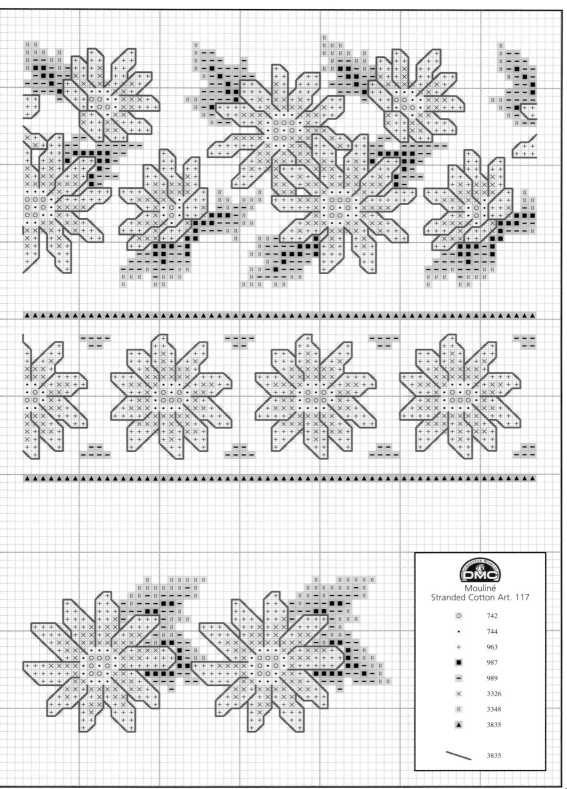

Mouliné
Stranded Cotton Art. 117

○	742
•	744
+	963
■	987
–	989
✕	3326
‖	3348
▲	3835
╱	3835

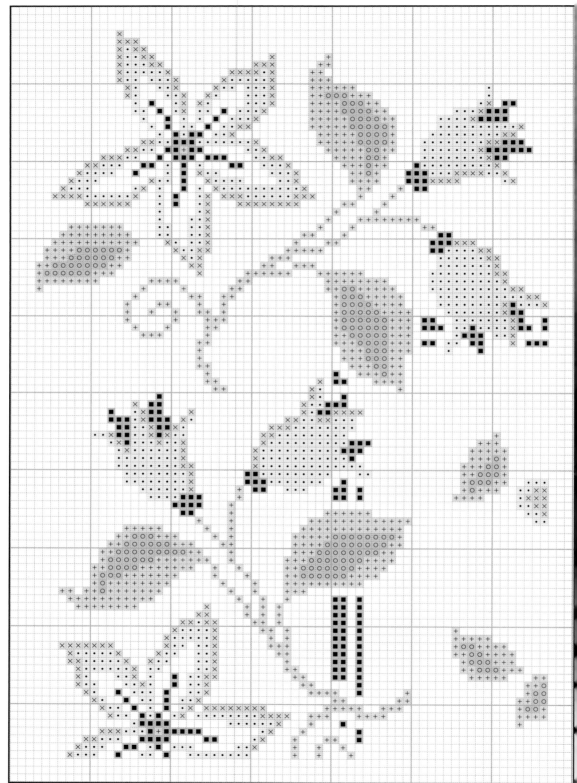

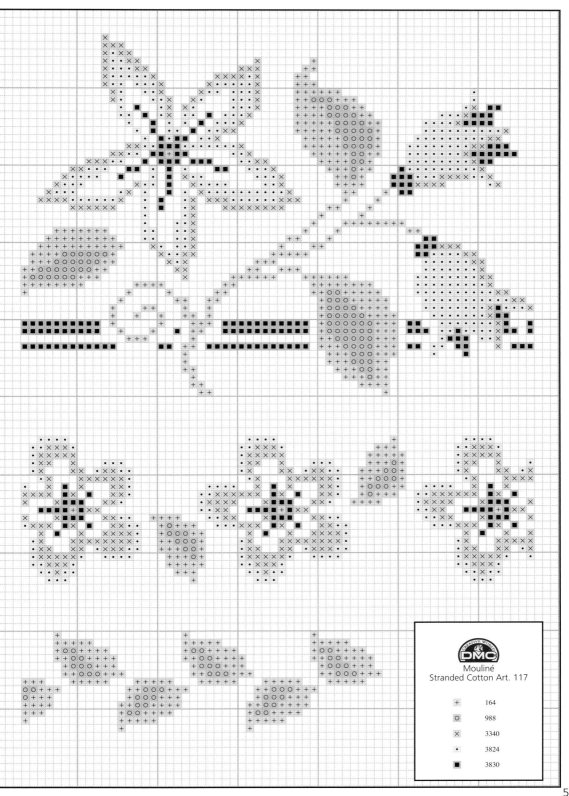

DMC
Mouliné
Stranded Cotton Art. 117

•	164
−	356
+	739
◎	988
✕	3766
■	3777
●	3815
T	3842

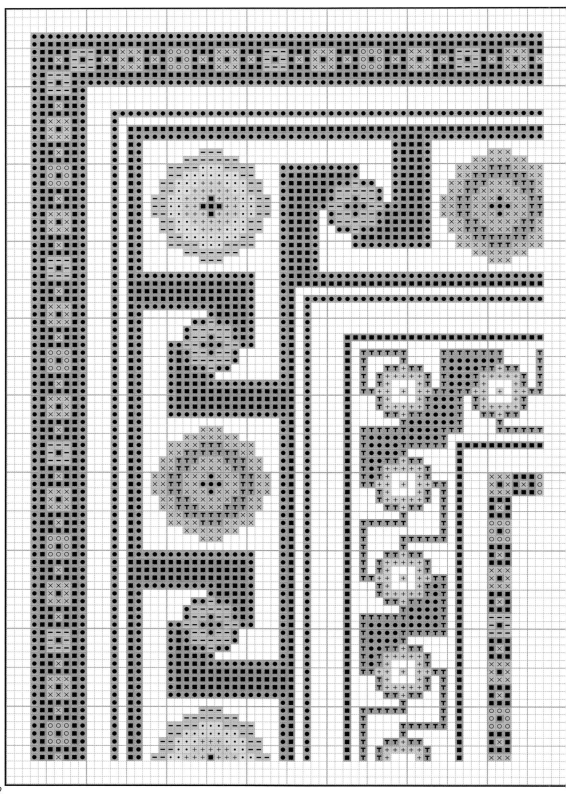

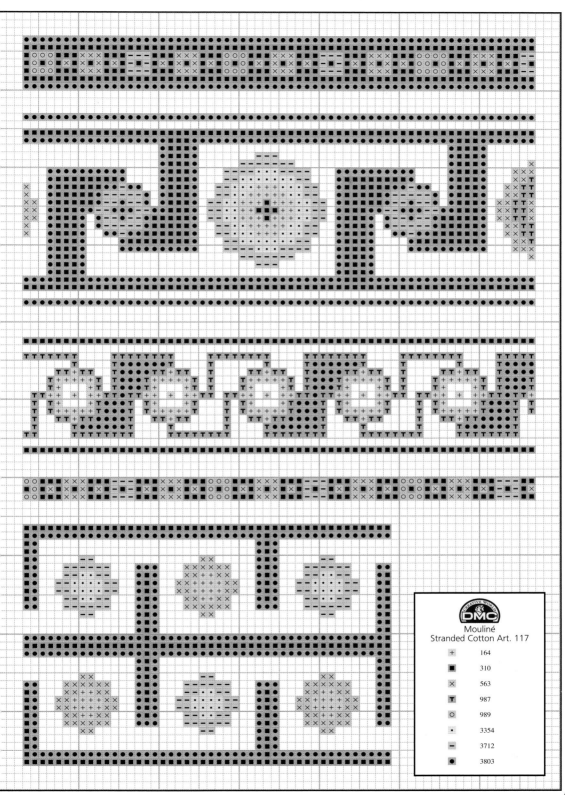

Mouliné
Stranded Cotton Art. 117

+	164
■	310
×	563
T	987
○	989
·	3354
−	3712
●	3803

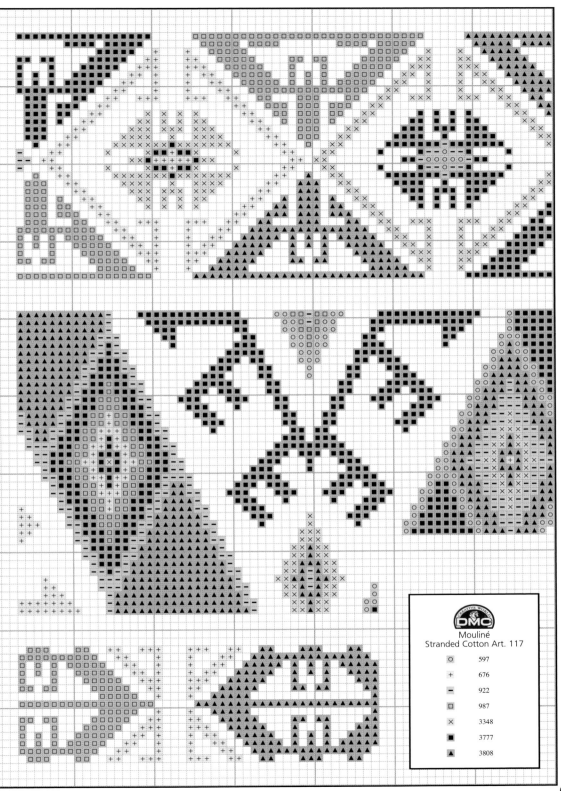

Mouliné
Stranded Cotton Art. 117

○	597
+	676
−	922
□	987
×	3348
■	3777
▲	3808

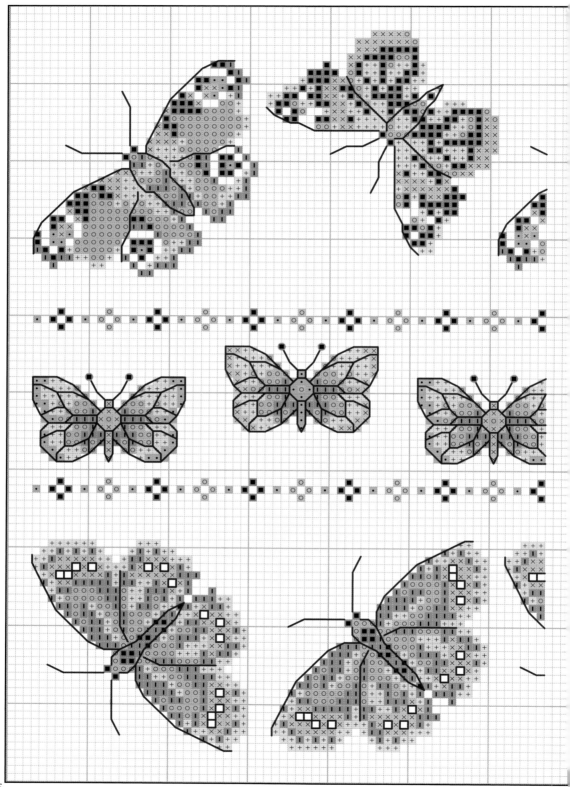

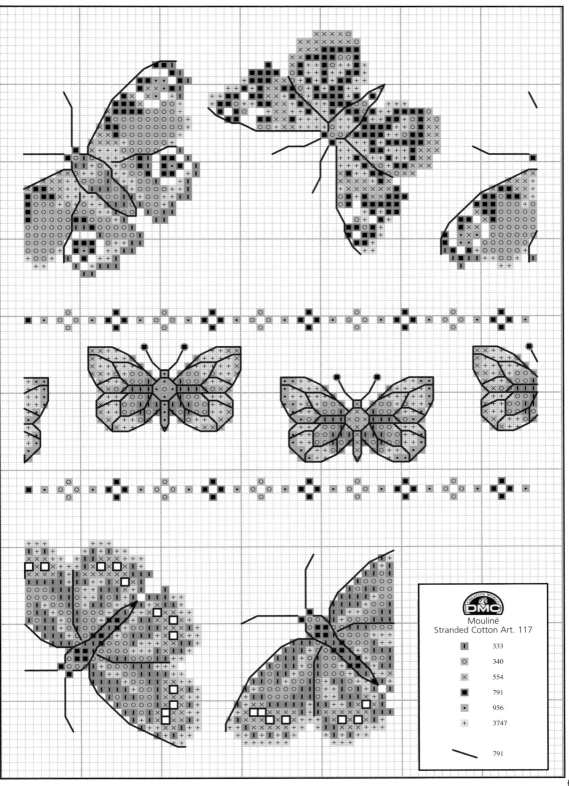

CREATIVE WORLD
DMC
Mouliné
Stranded Cotton Art. 117

I	333
O	340
X	554
■	791
·	956
+	3747
╱	791

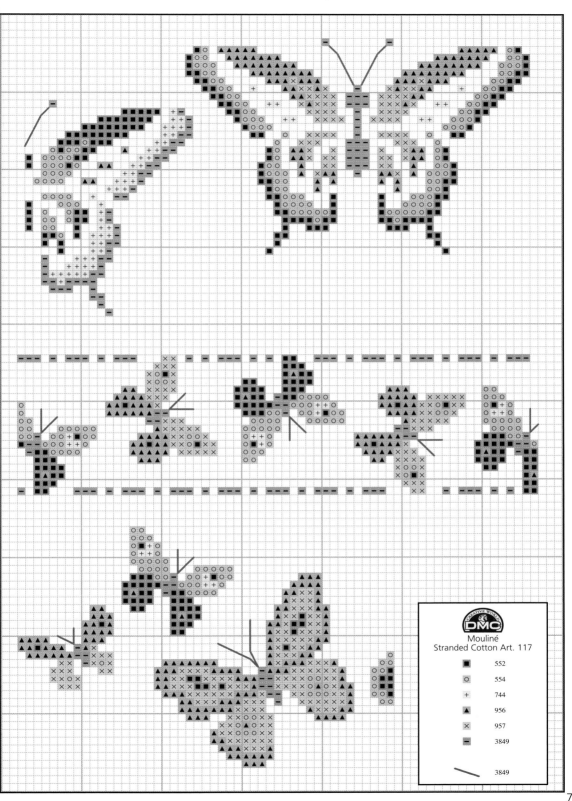

DMC
Mouliné
Stranded Cotton Art. 117

■	552
○	554
+	744
▲	956
✕	957
▬	3849
╱	3849

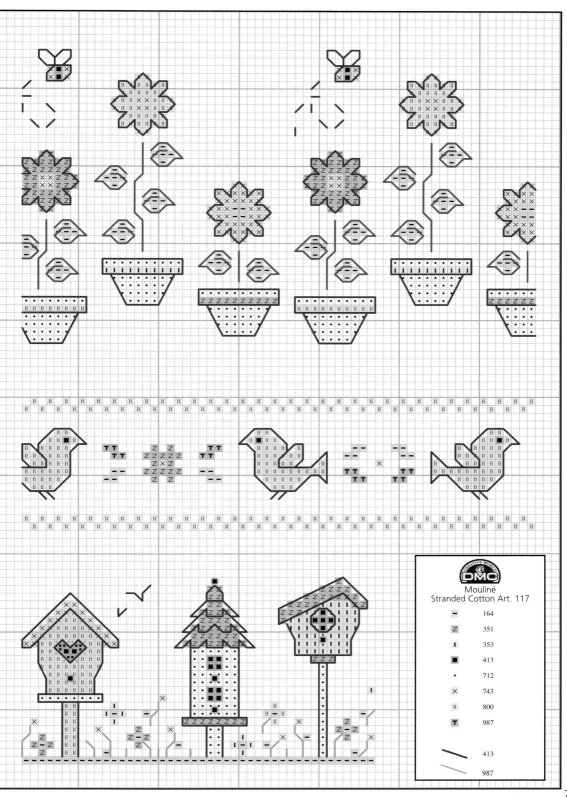

CREATIVE WORLD
DMC
Mouliné
Stranded Cotton Art. 117

−	164
Z	351
I	353
■	413
•	712
×	743
II	800
T	987
	413
	987

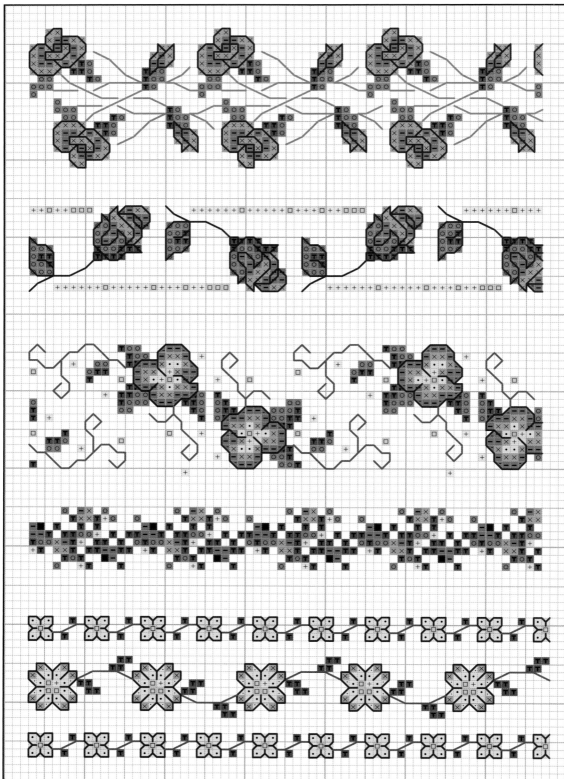

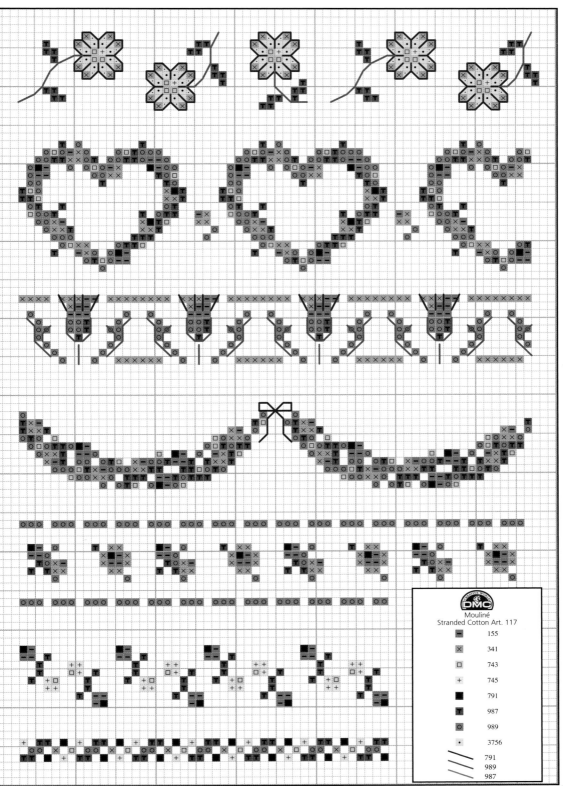

DMC
Mouliné
Stranded Cotton Art. 117

−	155
✕	341
□	743
+	745
■	791
T	987
◉	989
·	3756
╱	791
╱	989
╱	987

DMC
Mouliné
Stranded Cotton Art. 117

○	552
=	554
▽	702
U	704
■	777
↑	993
✕	3814
▲	3831
+	3833

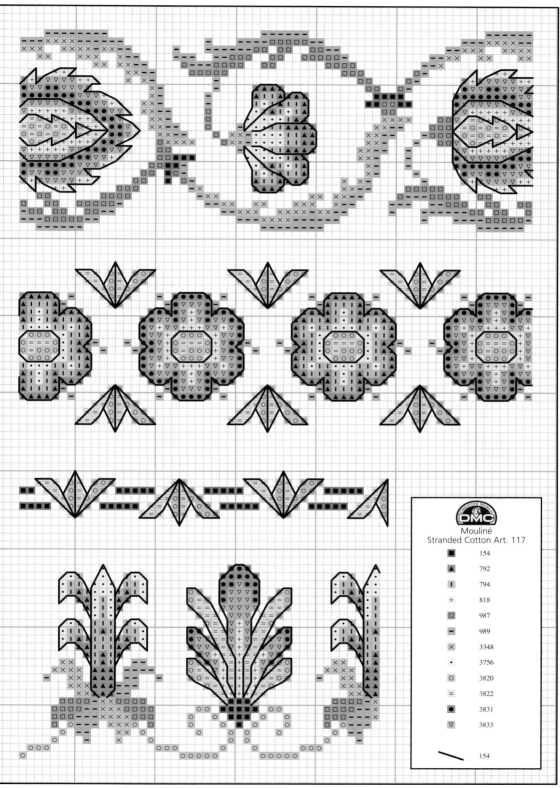

DMC
Mouliné
Stranded Cotton Art. 117

■	154
▲	792
I	794
+	818
▣	987
–	989
✕	3348
•	3756
○	3820
=	3822
●	3831
▽	3833
╱	154

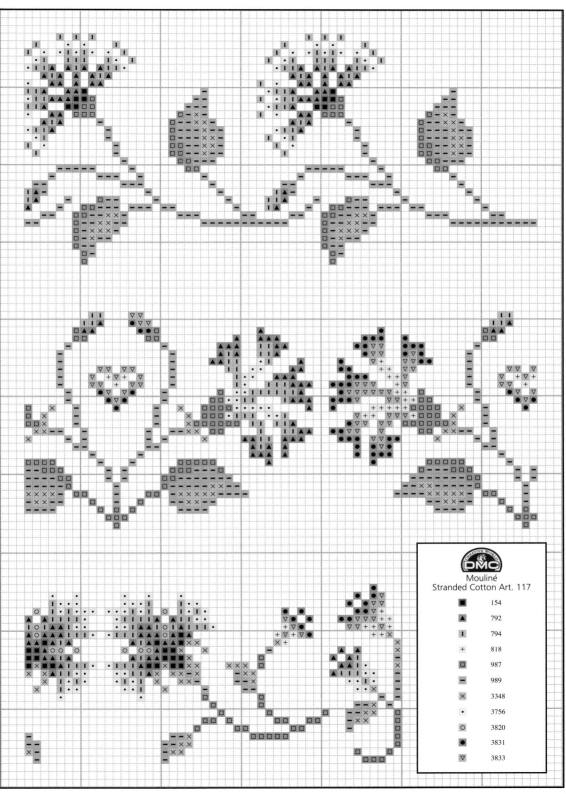

DMC
Mouliné
Stranded Cotton Art. 117

Symbol	Color
■	154
▲	792
I	794
+	818
▣	987
–	989
×	3348
·	3756
○	3820
●	3831
▽	3833

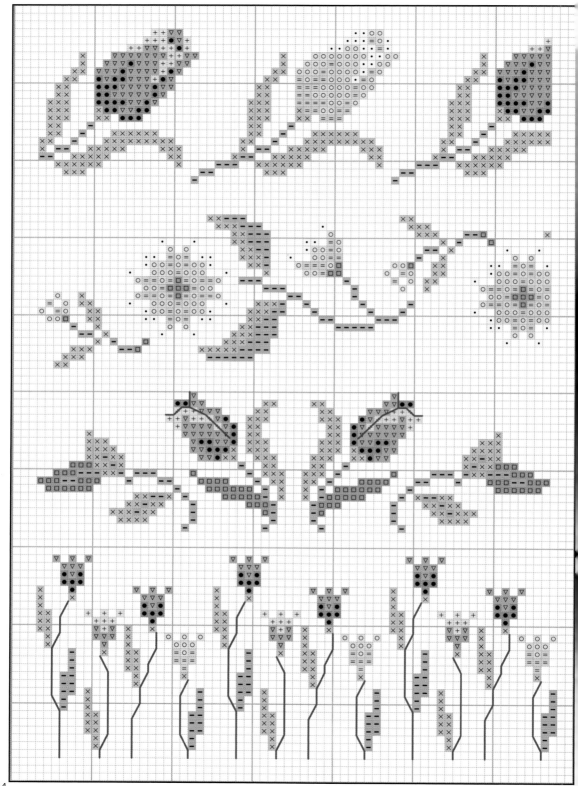

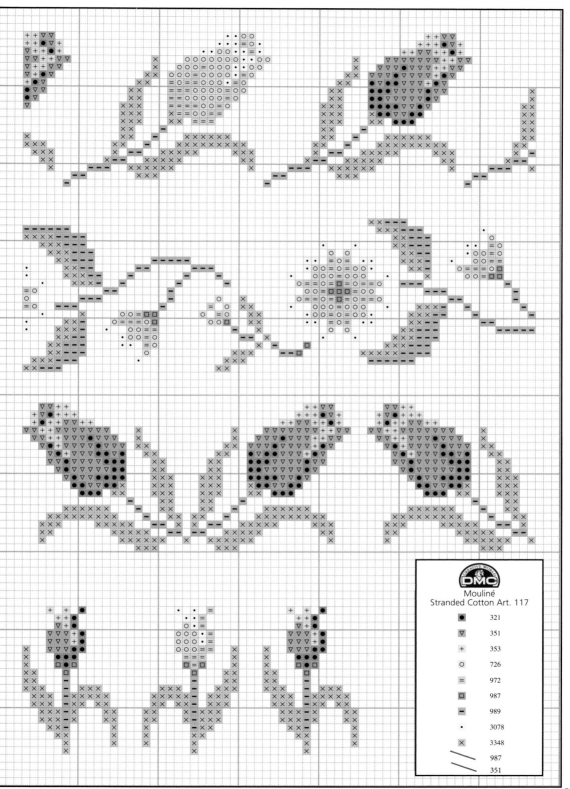

DMC
Mouliné
Stranded Cotton Art. 117

●	321
▽	351
+	353
○	726
=	972
▣	987
−	989
·	3078
×	3348
╱	987
╱	351

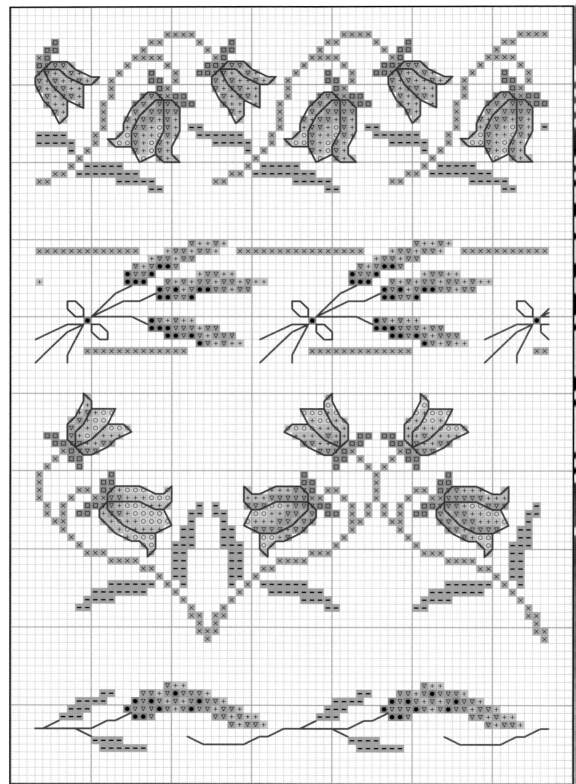

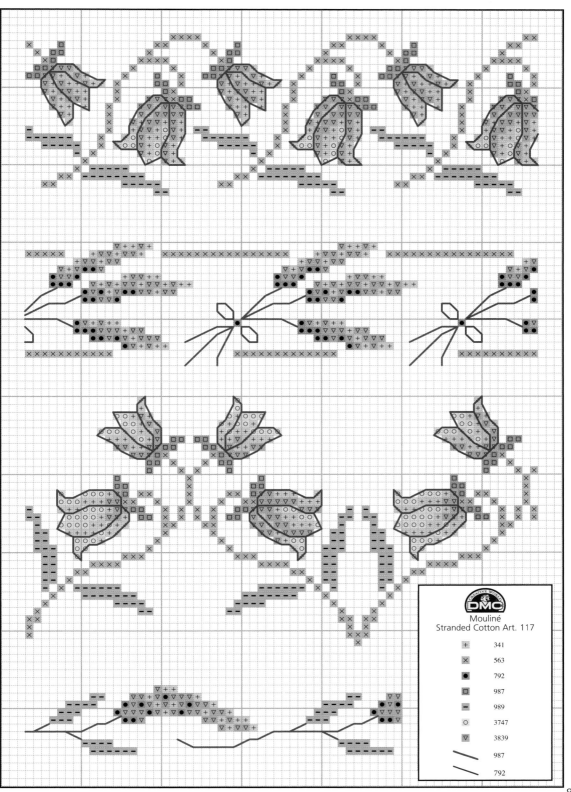

DMC
Mouliné
Stranded Cotton Art. 117

●	351
✕	563
·	967
▢	987
–	989
△	3341
✚	3777
/	3777
/	987

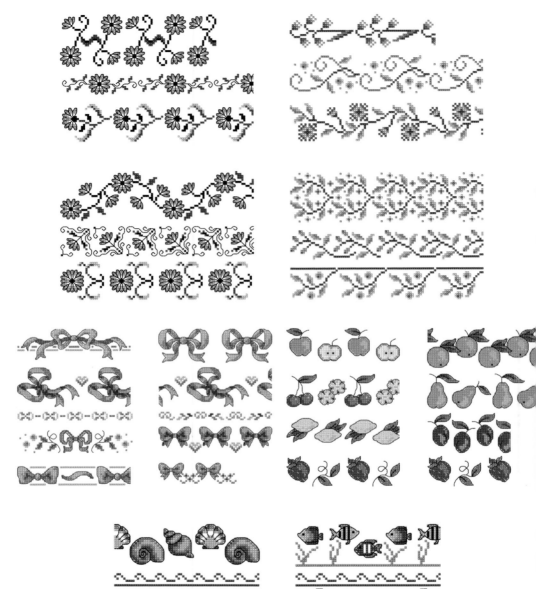

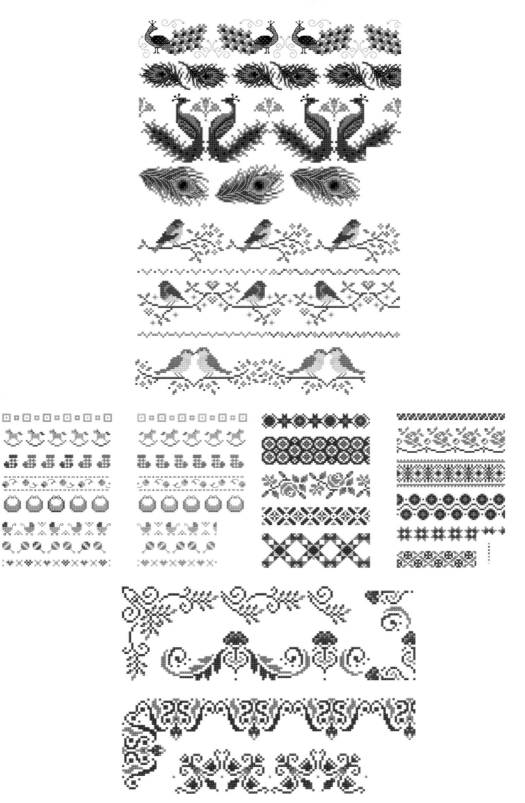

DMC
Mouliné
Stranded Cotton Art. 117

×	775
−	798
●	809
▣	823
╱	823

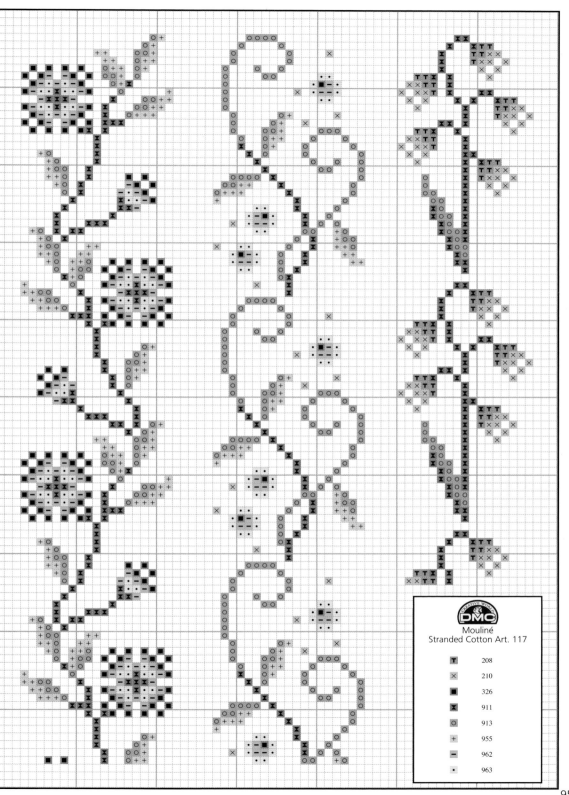

Mouliné
Stranded Cotton Art. 117

T	208
×	210
■	326
✗	911
⊙	913
+	955
−	962
·	963

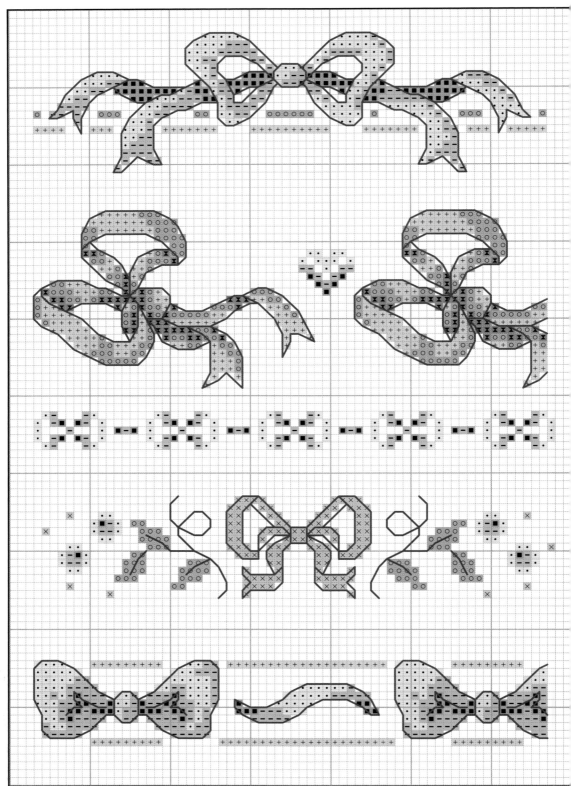

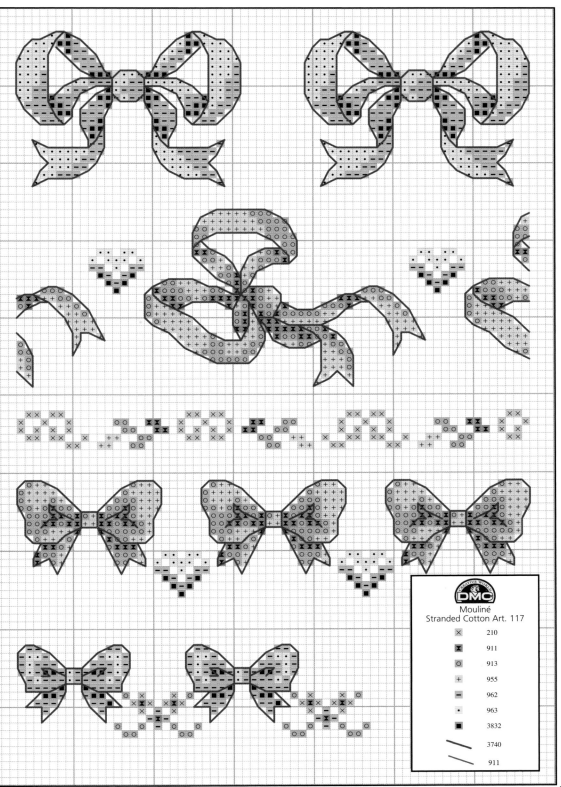

DMC
Mouliné
Stranded Cotton Art. 117

×	210
▣	911
◎	913
+	955
–	962
·	963
■	3832
╱	3740
╱	911

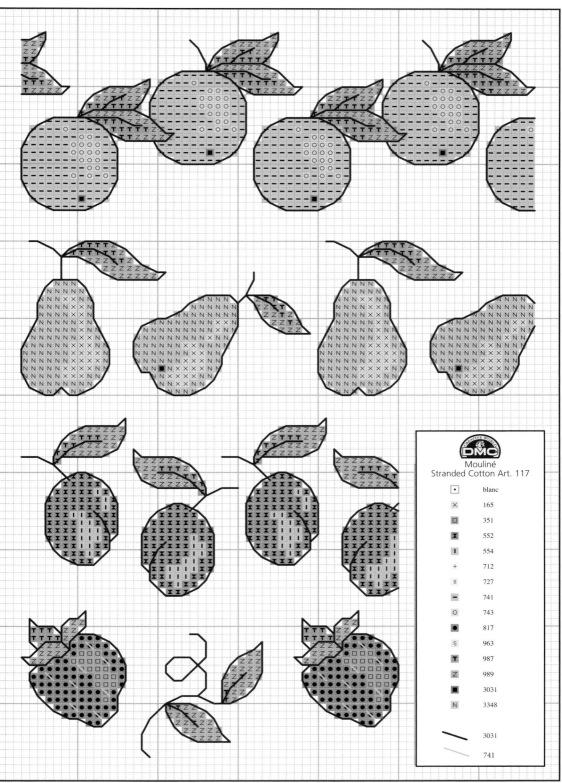

DMC
CREATIVE WORLD

Mouliné
Stranded Cotton Art. 117

·	blanc
×	165
□	351
⊠	552
I	554
+	712
‖	727
−	741
○	743
●	817
S	963
T	987
Z	989
■	3031
N	3348
╱	3031
╱	741

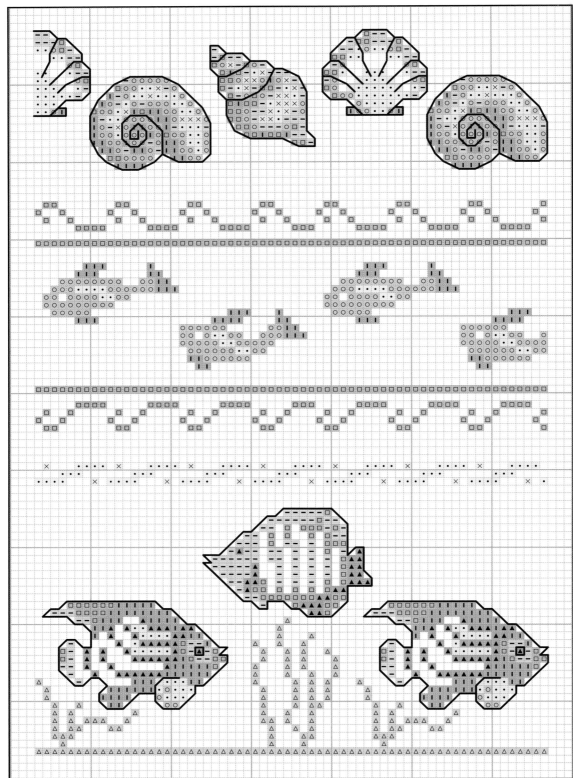

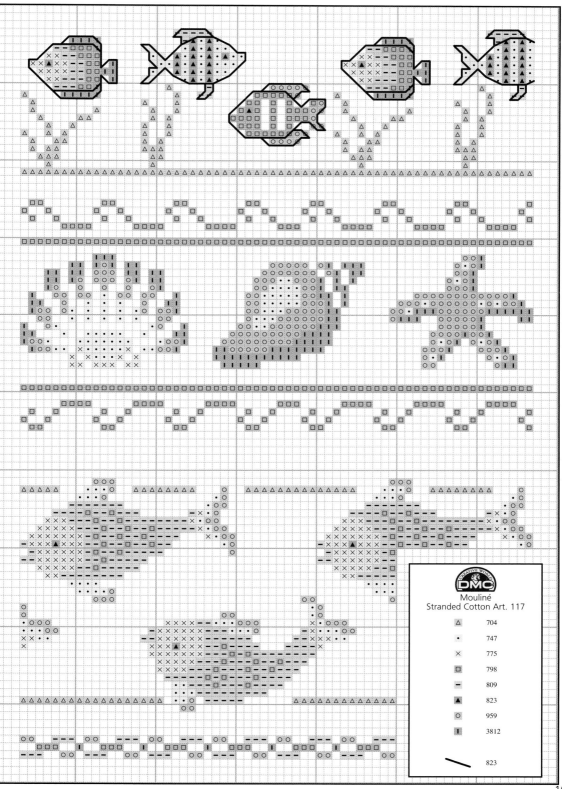

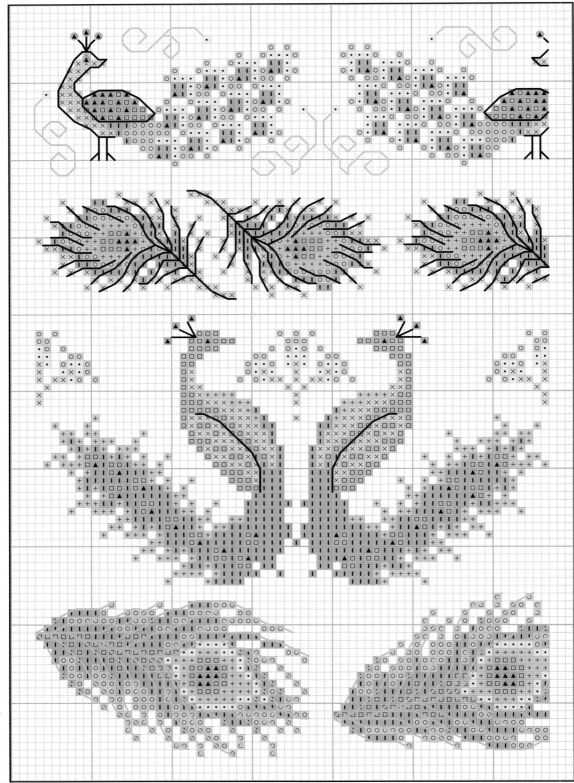

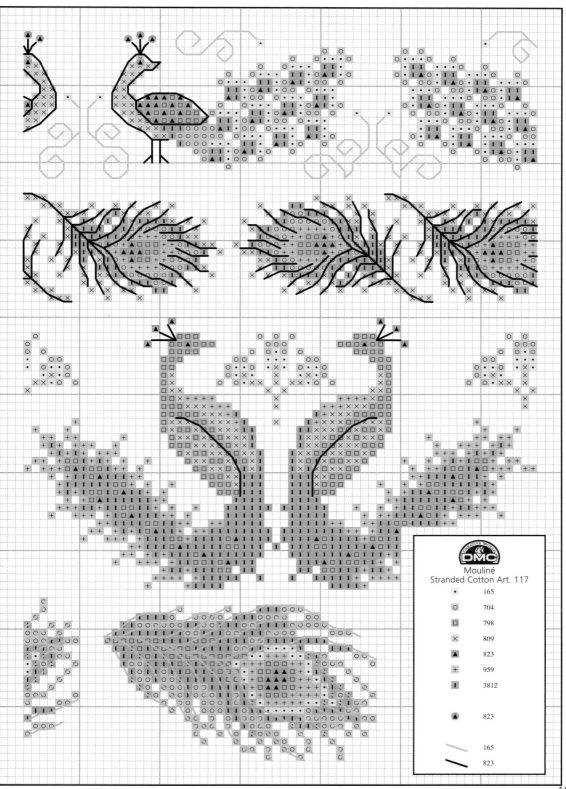

DMC
Mouliné
Stranded Cotton Art. 117

·	165
○	704
□	798
×	809
▲	823
+	959
I	3812
▲	823
╱	165
╱	823

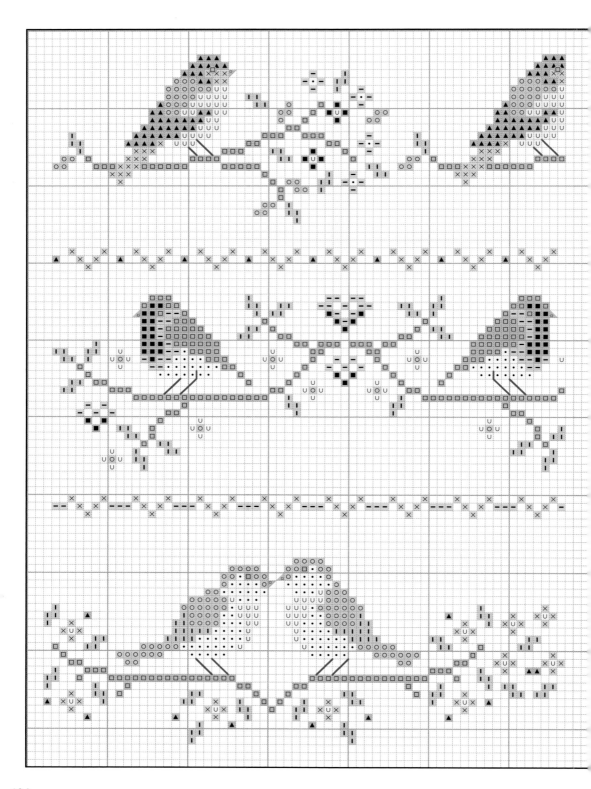

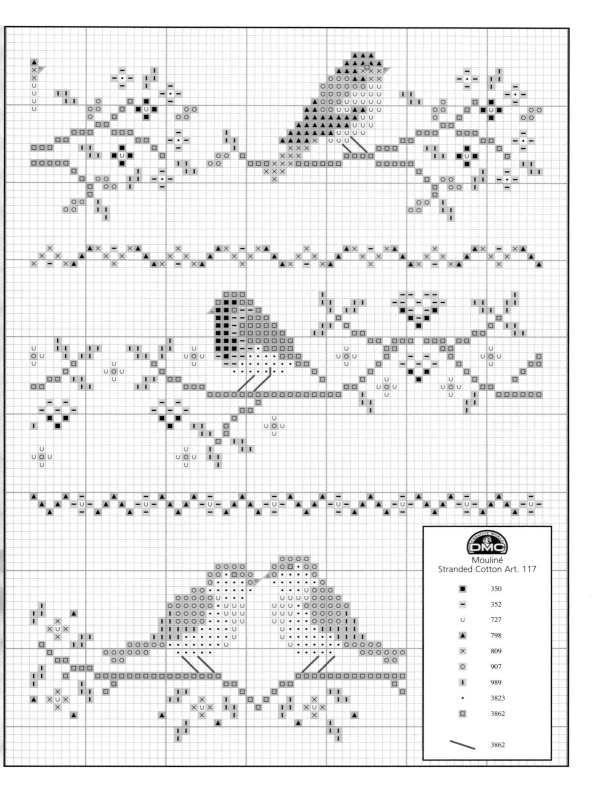

Mouliné
Stranded Cotton Art. 117

■	350
−	352
U	727
▲	798
✕	809
○	907
I	989
·	3823
□	3862
╱	3862

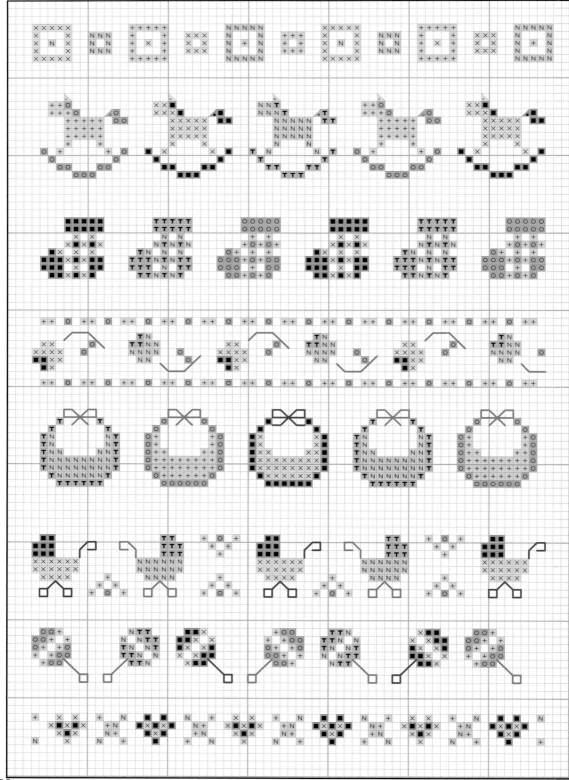

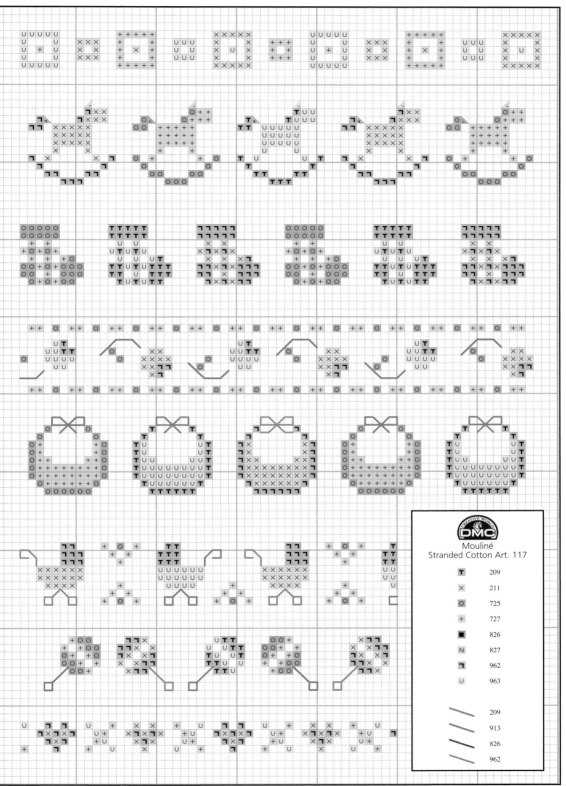

Mouliné
Stranded Cotton Art. 117

T	209
×	211
◎	725
+	727
■	826
N	827
⌐	962
U	963

╱	209
╱	913
╱	826
╱	962

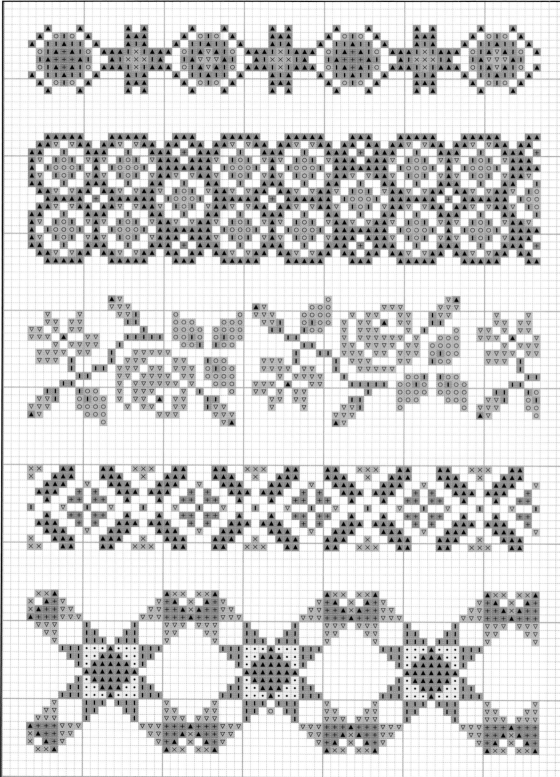

DMC
Mouliné
Stranded Cotton Art. 117

▽	152
▲	315
+	321
I	367
○	368
✕	704
·	745

Mouliné
Stranded Cotton Art. 117

▽	152
▲	315
+	321
I	367
○	368
✕	704

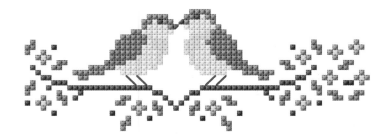